My Color-Full Florida

A fun and interactive way to learn about Florida's history

Written by Linda Schilling Mitchell
Illustrated by Jayne Maxwell Swartzwelder

Copyright © 2015 Linda Schilling Mitchell
All rights reserved.

ISBN: 1507586140
ISBN 13: 9781507586143

This book is dedicated to
Lydia, Abby, Jeffrey and Scarlett

Welcome to

My Color~Full Florida

Are you ready to explore the history that has made Florida such an interesting and colorful place?

Together we are going to learn about some of the people, places and things that make Florida a fascinating, unique place to live, and an exciting place to visit.

The following collection of stories strives to educate with historical and fun facts, and entertain with illustrations that can be colored if you desire.

So let's get started discovering My Color~Full Florida.

This book belongs to:

_____

Table Of Contents

Story	Page
Discovering Florida	1
The Saint Johns River	5
Lighthouses	9
House of Refuge	13
Barefoot Mailman	17
Flagler's Railway	21
The Over~Sea Railway	25
Florida Citrus	29
Pelicans	33
The Coral Castle	37
Ringling Museum of Art	41
Bok Tower Gardens	45
Cypress Gardens	49
Weeki Wachee Springs	53
Stephen Foster	57
Solomon's Castle	61
The Everglades	65
Fascinating Florida Facts	69
My Color-Full Florida Favorites	73

Discovering Florida
Feast of Flowers

Discovering Florida

Did you know that there were people living in Florida thousands of years ago? And did you know those people were Indians? Yes, there were several different tribes or groups of Indians living all around what is now the state of Florida. There were the Apachlachee, Timucua, Ais, Calusa, Tequesta Indians and others. Can you pronounce their names? Many of these Indians were fishermen and hunters, all living off what they could grow or catch in the different areas where they lived. But things were about to change because of a man named Juan Ponce de Leon.

Ponce de Leon was born in Spain in 1460. As a boy he was very smart, served as a messenger for the Royal Court, grew up to be a soldier, and loved adventure. In 1493, he sailed with explorer Christopher Columbus when the island of Puerto Rico was discovered. Eventually in the year 1509, he became the governor of Puerto Rico. The King of Spain encouraged Ponce de Leon to go explore other nearby islands. So in March of 1513, he and two hundred sailors left Puerto Rico in three ships to search for new lands, and especially the Islands of Benimy. They sailed for several days past many different islands in the Bahamas.

On April 2, 1513, Ponce de Leon spotted the island he was looking for. When he came ashore he named this new land *La Florida* because of the beautiful trees and flowers, and because it was during the celebration the Spaniards called Pascua Florida or Festival of Flowers. It's a perfect name don't you agree? The explorers stayed five days before returning to their ships and sailing further south. But in reality, Ponce de Leon hadn't discovered an island after all; it was the beautiful state of Florida. That's why in 2013, Florida celebrated its 500th anniversary. (1513-2013) Another very historic year for Florida.

Although we don't know the exact spot, it is believed that Ponce de Leon landed near St. Augustine. The actual *city* of St. Augustine was founded in 1565 by a Spanish Admiral named Pedro Menéndez de Avilés, and is the oldest city in the United States. There you can visit the oldest house, oldest school, and other historic buildings. You can even explore a massive fort.

To learn more about St. Augustine and see additional photos, visit www.augustine.com/history

The Saint Johns River

Florida's Lazy River

The Saint Johns River

Eleven thousand miles of rivers, streams and waterways flow through the state of Florida. As a result, rivers played an important part in Florida's early history. Most pioneer families settled close to the rivers because steamboats regularly brought needed supplies and visitors to the new towns.

Do you know which Florida River is the longest? That would be the St. Johns River which is approximately three hundred and ten miles long. Beginning in a swampy area of Indian River County and growing into a large river ending up in the Atlantic Ocean at the northern city of Jacksonville, it is different than most rivers. The St. Johns flows from the south to the north. And while many rivers have water reflecting shades of blue or green, the St. Johns' water is brown, looking more like ice tea. This comes from 'tannins', a natural color caused by decaying plant material.

The St. Johns River connects with hundreds of large and small lakes as it travels along the east coast of Florida. Numerous smaller rivers and creeks branch off from it, allowing boats to carry passengers to other inland towns. The St. Johns River has a nick name too. It is called the Lazy River because its water flows so slowly, creeping along at only one third mile per hour.

Years ago, as more towns sprung up along the river, tourists wanted to visit, especially in the winter when it was cold up north. Hotels were built for tourists and people moved into towns to start other businesses that the tourists would need or enjoy. Everyone wanted to come to Florida.

Over the years the river has been called many names. The native Timucua Indians called it *Welaka*, meaning River of Lakes. Spanish seamen change it to *Rio de Corrientes*, or River of Currents. The French built Fort Caroline and renamed it *Riviere de Mai,* or River of May because they arrived there on May 1st. Not liking this at all, the Spaniards captured the fort and then called the river *San Mateo.* Finally, the river was given the name *Rio de San Juan* after a mission near its mouth named San Juan del Puerto. This translates into English as the *St. Johns River* as we now know it.

Today people love to go boating, kayaking and canoeing on the St. Johns River and all the lakes and tributaries along its path. Is that something you would like to do?

Lighthouses

Lighthouse, lighthouse
Tall and bright,
Guiding ships by day and night.
Helping them know where to be,
As they sail your patch of sea.

Lighthouses

Have you ever seen a lighthouse? They have a very important job, you know. Lighthouses stand guard day and night, every day of the year, perched high on rocky cliffs or on sandy sea shores. A lighthouse uses its bright light to warn sailors on ships that they need to stay a safe distance away from where the lighthouse is located. That's so the ships or boats won't run aground or crash into nearby rocks. They also help the sailors know where the inlets are so they can pass through safely.

There are thirty remaining historic lighthouses along the state's 1,350 mile coastline. As you stand on the ground and gaze upward, you feel miniature in comparison with the towering concrete or brick columns stretching high towards the sky above you.

The first lighthouse in Florida was a Spanish watchtower built in St. Augustine in the late 1500's. The current one hundred and sixty five foot tall lighthouse was built in 1874 on a location nearby. The shortest lighthouse is in Key West, with only eighty-eight steps to the top, and is now a museum. The tallest is Ponce de Leon Inlet lighthouse, soaring one-hundred and seventy-five feet high with a challenging two hundred and three step climb to the top. Would you like to climb to the top of a lighthouse?

Each lighthouse is painted with different designs and colors. That way the sailors out at sea during the day can recognize where they are by how the lighthouse looks. At night the bright light from the lighthouse can help sailors determine where they are too. Even though it appears to flash, the light is a steady beam but flashes as it rotates by in a circle. The timing between flashes is different for each lighthouse so the sailors can tell which lighthouse it is by the amount of time between flashes.

Years ago the light used oil for fuel. The lighthouse keeper had to climb up all the steps to the top carrying buckets of the heavy oil. He also had to make sure the lens and windows were clean, and make sure all the gears worked smoothly. Every day and night, in all types of weather, the lighthouse keeper worked hard to keep all the ships safe.

More interesting information about Florida lighthouses can be found at:
www.lighthousefriends.com/fl.htm

House of Refuge
Last House Standing

House Of Refuge

Back in 1876 under direction of the U.S. Treasury Department, the United States Life Saving Service started building ten special houses in different places along Florida's coast. Each House of Refuge provided food, clothing and a safe place to stay for survivors of shipwrecks and storms at sea. If you were on a ship and it sank, wouldn't you be happy to have a House of Refuge to stay in until someone could pick you up and take you back home? They weren't very fancy buildings, and they all looked alike. Built of strong Florida pine wood, the main floor was divided into four rooms – a kitchen, dining room, living room and a bedroom used by the Keeper of the House. The Keeper of the House was hired to care for the stranded sailors. If he was married, his wife was in charge of cooking meals for everyone and caring for their clothes. Upstairs was one large room with twenty beds where the shipwreck survivors could sleep. A big porch wrapped all the way around the building, which would keep the house shaded from the hot sun, because there was no air conditioning back then.

Another very important job the Keeper of the House had was to keep a detailed log or journal. He wrote down the names of the sailors who stayed there, when they arrived, and when they left, and any other important things that happened. He had to make entries in this log every day.

All of the House of Refuge buildings are gone except the one built in 1876 located on Hutchinson Island in Stuart, Florida. The building has sat high on a rocky ledge overlooking the ocean for more than one hundred and thirty-five years. A tall lookout tower was built during World War II and also remains standing.

Today *The House of Refuge at Gilbert's Bar* is a historic landmark and museum. It has displays of life saving equipment used over the years, and you can tour the interior of the house and see the way it looked in 1904. You will also see the beautiful, hand-written entries in the log dating back to 1879. It's fun to stand inside the house or on the porch and wonder what it must have been like for those sailors who stayed there so long ago.

Want to learn more about The House of Refuge? Visit www.houseofrefugefl.org

Barefoot Mailman
Brave & Hearty Men

Barefoot Mailman

Do you like to get mail? We all enjoy going to the mailbox and finding cards or letters from friends and family. Can you imagine waiting six to eight weeks to get a letter? That's how long it took years ago for a letter to go only sixty-eight miles from Palm Beach to Miami. But then along came the *Barefoot Mailman* who would walk the long trip every week. Just think how happy people were to see him bringing their letters so quickly.

One of the first Barefoot Mailmen was Edward Ruthven Bradley, and he walked the mail one hundred and thirty-six miles round trip each week. It was such a hard trip that Edward and his son Louie would take turns doing the route, often walking barefoot along the beach. Picture yourself doing that in the hot summers during storms with mosquitoes and possibly alligators all around while carrying a heavy sack of mail.

Each and every Monday, Edward or Louie would leave Palm Beach, row a boat to the edge of Lake Worth, and then walk to the Orange Grove House of Refuge in Delray Beach where he spent the night. The next day he walked twenty five miles, crossed the Hillsboro Inlet by row boat, and then traveled by foot to the New River House of Refuge in Fort Lauderdale where he spent that night. On Wednesday he would row a boat down to the south side of the New River Inlet, walk the beach again for ten miles, reaching Baker's Haulover at the head of Biscayne Bay. Another ride by row boat took him down the bay to the post office at Miami. After spending the night in Miami, he left Thursday for his return to Palm Beach by Saturday afternoon. Round trip involved eighty miles on foot and fifty six miles by boat.

Historic research shows twenty different men held the job as Barefoot Mailman from 1885 to 1893. That's when a rock road was completed and the mail could be carried more quickly and easily by wagon or stage coach.

Because their role was so important in Florida's history, a bronze statue of the Barefoot Mailman is located near the Hillsboro Inlet and pays tribute to those brave and hearty men.

For more information about the Barefoot Mailman, be sure to visit www.en.wikipedia.org/wiki/Barefoot_mailman

Flagler's Railway
Opening Florida to the World

Flagler's Railway

Do you like trains? So do I, and so did a man named Henry Morrison Flagler. Henry was born in 1830, and grew up to be a very smart and very wealthy businessman. He first visited Florida in 1878 when he brought his wife to Jacksonville so she could feel better in the warm sunshine. He returned to Florida again in 1883, this time staying in St. Augustine. He loved the city and the weather, but he was not impressed with the hotels there at the time. Being the smart businessman that he was, he knew other people would love to come to Florida also, especially wealthy tourists wanting to stay in fancy new hotels.

So Henry Flagler went to work having a beautiful, elegant hotel with five-hundred forty rooms built called The Ponce de Leon. It was bigger and better than any hotel in the area, and it was an instant success. He also built the Alcazar Hotel across the street, which had a huge indoor swimming pool and other recreational activities. Everyone wanted to stay at The Ponce de Leon and Alcazar.

Now Henry figured if people liked visiting St. Augustine, they would like to visit other areas of Florida, especially places farther south where the weather was even warmer. But how would they get there, and where would they stay?

Many tourists traveled by steamboats to towns along the rivers back then. But Henry knew people would love to be near the ocean. He decided to build a railway with train stations all along the coast. His next stop for his railway was in Ormond Beach where he purchased the Ormond Hotel in 1891. His railway continued on to West Palm Beach where he built the Royal Poinciana Hotel in 1894 and the Breakers Hotel in 1896.

Henry thought he was finished once he got to West Palm Beach, but people in south Florida talked him into bringing his train all the way down to Miami. The train would not only bring tourists to Miami to visit, but it would carry produce such as oranges, pineapples, and vegetables back up north on its return trips. He continued his Florida East Coast Railway south, and opened his Royal Palm Hotel in Miami in 1897.

By now Henry was sixty-seven years old and had worked very hard for a very long time. Do you think he was ready to stop? Let's read our next story...

The Over~Sea Railway
Flagler's Folly

The Over~Sea Railway

What do you think? Did Henry Flagler stop building his railway once he got to Miami? If you guessed NO, you would be right.

Henry was seventy-four years old in 1904 when he decided the railway should continue another one-hundred fifty-six miles, all the way down to Key West. He knew this was a good idea because huge ships would be bringing products into Key West. The trains could now quickly carry those products all the way to New York and other places. The train could also bring tourists down to Key West to enjoy the warm, sunny weather.

How would he build tracks over the water between so many small islands in the Keys? Many people even laughed at Henry, and some called his project Flagler's Folly. But he was determined, so he hired several very smart men to help him figure out a way.

It took a great deal of research and planning to come up with methods to connect the many islands. Dirt mounds called causeways were built over areas where the water was shallow, but over the deeper parts, they had to build bridges. Some of the spans were made of concrete, low across the water. Another section was made of steel and built high above the water. The biggest challenge was a seven mile section over the water. It took five-hundred forty-six concrete piers to make this section of the bridge, the longest open portion of the route.

For eight years, thousands of workers spent long days working on the bridges and laying the railway tracks. They worked fourteen hours a day, six days a week for $1.50 a day. There were mosquitoes and hurricanes making it even harder. Finally on January 22, 1912, eighty-two year old Henry Flagler and his wife Mary Lily rode the first train on the Key West Over-Sea Railway. How excited and happy he must have been!

The trains continued traveling to and from Key West until the railway tracks suffered damaged during a 1935 hurricane. In 1938 the railway was changed into a highway for cars to cross from Miami to Key West. It was now called the Over-Sea Highway. Eventually, because of the increase of traffic to the lower Keys, new bridges with wider lanes were built from 1978-1982.

Would you like to take a ride on the bridge all the way to Key West?

Florida Citrus

Sunshine in a Glass

Florida Citrus

Citrus: Oranges, grapefruit, tangerines, lemons, limes and more. Doesn't everyone like some or all of it? But even though the orange blossom is Florida's state flower, citrus wasn't always in Florida. The origin or beginning of citrus goes back to tropical Southeast Asia or the country of Malaysia today. Citrus fruits were enjoyed by royalty and common people alike in ancient China and later in Japan and the South Pacific. The people also liked the pretty fragrance of the flowers.

Over time, merchants and explorers carried citrus seeds to places such as Greece and Rome. Florida's citrus came with the first Spanish and Portuguese explorers. The Portuguese explorers found an especially sweet orange in India which they quickly named the "Portuguese Orange". In 1493, Christopher Columbus brought lemon, lime, and orange seeds to an island once called Hispaniola, which we know today as Haiti and the Dominican Republic. Juan Ponce de Leon, who discovered Florida, lived there during that time. Many believe he carried some of the citrus seeds with him when he discovered Florida in 1513.

Florida's weather and sandy soil were perfect for growing citrus. By 1579, orange trees were growing all around St. Augustine, and in time, it was the main crop for the early pioneer settlers.

A Frenchman, named Odet Philippe brought the grapefruit from the West Indies to Florida, planting the first grove near Tampa in 1823.

As the citrus business grew, so did Florida. The ability to grow citrus inland from the coastal areas led to further development of the state and, as the railroads expanded, trains carried citrus to other parts of the country. Florida led the nation's citrus industry, and even today, it is one of the main industries in Florida.

We want to thank explorers like Christopher Columbus, Ponce de Leon, Philippe and others for the chain of events that brought citrus not only to Florida, but to the entire country. So the next time you pour a glass of orange juice, cut open a grapefruit, or slip a slice of lemon into your tea, think about the long journey citrus has taken over the years. Right to your breakfast table!

Pelicans
Old Joe

Pelicans

There is an abundance of beautiful birds throughout Florida. Over five-hundred different types of birds love to live here because of our warm climate, various water supplies, and variety of food.

One favorite bird is the Brown Pelican. You will often see them flying low and slow over the waves in the ocean. The Brown Pelican is the smallest of the pelican species even though they average four- feet long, weigh eight to ten pounds, and have a wingspan of six to seven feet. Their legs are short and all four toes are webbed. Their uniquely designed bill is eighteen inches long and includes a large pouch or "gular" with an amazing three gallon capacity. Once a fish is caught, the pouch drains out the water, the pelican tosses his head back and gulp, the fish is swallowed whole.

The Brown Pelicans have the dare-devil habit of plunging headfirst from heights of thirty to sixty feet into the water to catch their fish. To watch this you have to wonder how they survive or keep from scrambling their little brains. But their heads are specially designed with tiny air sacs (frontal air bags perhaps) just beneath the skin to soften the impact. This design is tested repeatedly as the large birds consume approximately four pounds of fish each day during a normal lifespan of thirty years.

The Brown Pelican's football-shaped body is covered with feathers, brownish-gray and darker on the undersides. When they mature, they have white heads crowned with yellow. During breeding season the throat becomes a chestnut color and a yellow patch appears at the base of the neck. If you're ever able to get close enough, you'll see that the color of a Pelican's eyes is striking, because the irises are often sky-blue and ringed in pink.

A very social bird, the Brown Pelicans congregate in flocks. As groups, they seem to especially enjoy gliding on the thermals in their squadron-like "V" formations. They usually have one brood (or litter) a year numbering two to three eggs. As good parents they share the responsibilities of nesting and caring for their young. Baby Pelicans are a fluffy, lighter brown color and often learn to swim before they can fly.

Would you like to learn more about Pelicans? You can by visiting www.en.wikipedia.org/wiki/Pelican

The Coral Castle
A Labor of Love

The Coral Castle

Can you imagine a castle made of coral? What if it wasn't a castle at all, but a large garden full of huge, carved pieces of coral rock? That's the kind of Coral Castle a man named Edward Leedskalnin built.

Edward moved to America from Europe because the cold weather there bothered his health. Plus Edward was very sad because his girlfriend Agnes had decided not to marry him. But by 1918 his health was better, so he moved to Florida City and purchased one acre of land to build his beautiful garden he called Rock Gate Park. Many believe he built it for Agnes, hoping she would be impressed with his labor of love and come back to him.

This was quite a big project for Edward who was less than five-feet tall and weighed just one hundred pounds. People often wonder how he was able to move the giant pieces of coral. Always working alone and at night using simple tools, Edward cut, carved, and moved TONS of coral stone, approximately 1,100 tons of stone in all, with some pieces weighing over fifty tons. He placed each one exactly where he wanted them in his garden.

Some of the stone sculptures he created included an enormous working sundial which towers twenty-five feet in the air, a BBQ, water well, fountain, beds and a bathtub. Furniture including a 5,000 pound heart shaped table, a table shaped like the state of Florida, twenty-five chairs, and rocking chairs that rock with ease. He even built a throne.

Then one day Edward decided to move all his massive sculptures. Can you imagine moving all those huge rocks? Again he did it alone and at night. And again we wonder how he did it. He would never tell anyone. The move took him over three years to complete. The new site had much more space so Edward could build even more sculptures. He built a large stone wall around the garden with his house located on top.

Edward worked on his special garden for twenty eight years. In time it was sold, and the new owners changed the name to The Coral Castle and opened it up for all people to see and enjoy. What a magical place to visit.

You can see pictures of Edward's amazing sculptures at www.coralcastle.com

Ringling Museum of Art
Greatest Show on Earth

Ringling Museum Of Art

Have you ever been to the circus? Animals doing tricks, funny clowns, acrobats and more, all under the direction of a lively Ringmaster decked out in a top hat and fancy jacket. It's exciting isn't it? A man named John Ringling also loved the circus. He was called the "King of the Big Top" and was the famous owner of "The Greatest Show on Earth".

John Ringling was born in 1866 and had six brothers and one sister. His four brothers started the Ringling Brothers Circus in 1884. By the time that he was eighteen years old, John was performing in the family circus as a song and dance man. Eventually, his brothers bought another circus company, The Barnum & Bailey Circus, and John was put in charge of running that circus. These two companies known as The Ringling Brothers, Barnum & Bailey Circus was called "The Greatest Show on Earth" in 1919.

In time, John and his wife Mable decided to spend the winter months in Sarasota, Florida. In 1924 they bought sixty-six acres of land and built a huge mansion with forty-one rooms and fifteen bathrooms. They named their palace *Ca' d'Zan* or House of John.

John traveled all over the world with his circus business. He and Mable enjoyed collecting huge amounts of art work, sculptures and paintings. Since he was now one of the richest men in the world, they could afford anything they wanted. As a result, a twenty-one room museum of art was built in 1927 to hold all their wonderful treasures.

However, his circus business started to fail because of the economic times of the Great Depression. By 1929 all he had left of his huge fortune was his home and his art collection. When John died in 1936, he gave his mansion, museum and art collection to the State of Florida. It is now operated as The John and Mable Ringling Museum of Art.

You can visit John and Mable's home and walk through the many rooms and see the splendor and wealth that was popular during a time in history known as the *Gilded Age*. There is a Circus Museum and the magnificent Historic Asolo Theater. This palace playhouse was built in 1798 in Asolo, Italy. In the mid 1950's, the theater was carefully taken apart and brought to the Ringling estate in Sarasota. Performances still take place there today.

Would you like to see the beautiful pictures of the theater and museum? There are many on their website at www.ringling.org

Bok Tower Gardens

"Make you the world a bit better

or more beautiful

because you have lived in it"

...Edward Bok

Bok Tower Gardens

Close your eyes. Feel the cool breeze on your face mixed with the tingle of warm sunshine. Breathe in the fragrance of fresh flowers as you enjoy the gentle songs of distant songbirds. Ah, is this a delightful dream? Go ahead, open your eyes. It's the beautiful Bok Tower Gardens.

Edward W. Bok was born on October 9, 1863 in the Netherlands. At the age of six, he came to America with his parents and older brother. He went to school in Brooklyn, New York and once he graduated, he went to work for different companies that published magazines. He was very good at his work and by the time he was twenty-one, he was the editor of *The Brooklyn Magazine.* By 1889, he moved to Philadelphia and was editor of *The Ladies Home Journal,* one of the most popular magazines in America. He also became a Pulitzer Prize winning author.

In 1896, Edward married Mary Louise Curtis. They spent their winters in the warm Florida climate just north of Lake Wales, in an area known as Mountain Lake Estates. During their walks they enjoyed the beauty of all the native flowers and trees. They loved it so much that they decided to purchase two-hundred and fifty acres of land to preserve as a garden and bird sanctuary. Thousands of subtropical garden trees and bushes were planted as a welcome invitation to hundreds of bird species to take up residence in a place of beauty and peace, just as Edward had envisioned.

Still something was missing. After thinking back to his early childhood in the Netherlands, he realized that the enchanting sounds of a carillon were just the added touch the gardens needed. A carillon is set of stationary bells or chimes hung in a tower and played by a person on a keyboard. That person is called a "carillonneur". Construction began in 1927 on the two-hundred and five foot tall, pink Georgia marble, neo Gothic inspired Singing Tower. Perched on top of Iron Mountain, the majestic tower can be seen from miles around. Bok's Singing Tower carillon, considered one of the best in the world, has sixty bells weighing between sixteen pounds and twelve tons. Can you imagine how beautiful they must sound?

We can still visit Bok Tower Gardens today and enjoy the beautiful flowers and trees in the gardens created by Edward and Mary Louise. And we can listen to live concerts on the carillon. We might even see the ducks and swans swimming among the lilies in the reflection pool in front of the Tower. What a beautiful place for them to live.

There is more to learn about Bok Tower Gardens at www.boktowergardens.org

Cypress Gardens
Past & Present

Cypress Gardens
Now Legoland

What would you think if your parents decided to move to Florida and turn sixteen acres of swampy land into a flower garden and tourist's attraction? That's exactly what Dick and Julie Pope did. They put their imagination, and ambition to work creating what is considered to be one of Florida's first commercial theme parks.

On January 2, 1936, Cypress Gardens opened to the public. It included over eight thousand varieties of flowers from over ninety countries decorating the landscape.

One favorite feature of Cypress Gardens was the lovely and graceful Southern Belles in their sun bonnets and large hoop skirt dresses. They would sit among the flowers by the gazebo or stroll along walkways in their beautiful gowns. Every little girl dreamed of growing up to be a beautiful Cypress Garden's Southern Belle one day.

Exciting water skiing shows were held with several people skiing together at once. At times they performed with large flags or standing on each other's shoulders, and forming what was known as the Human Pyramid. Their daring jumps and spins thrilled everyone in the audience.

Sadly, Cypress Gardens could not compete with the newer attractions in Orlando and elsewhere around the state. Damage from hurricanes and a drop in visits by tourists caused the once-famous Cypress Gardens to close in September, 2009.

But that's not the end of our story. On January 15, 2010 Merlin Entertainment purchased the Cypress Gardens site with the plans to build their fifth Legoland Park. Today as the largest of all the Legoland parks, it is divided into eleven separate sections with over fifty rides, shows and attractions specifically designed for visitors aged two to twelve years, where everyone in the family becomes a hero. It covers one hundred and forty five acres and includes a section of the historic Cypress Gardens as part of the park. The Triple Hurricane Roller Coaster is one of the original attractions that was kept and restored. The original gazebo has also been restored, and even Lego Southern Belles grace the gardens, all paying proper respect to its famous predecessor, Cypress Gardens.

Does Legoland sound like a fun place for you to visit? Find out more about it at www.florida.legoland.com

Weeki Wachee Springs
Mermaids & More

Weeki Wachee Springs

Do you believe in Mermaids? Apparently a man named Newton Perry did.

Years ago, back before there was Disney World, Florida had many roadside attractions. Located along the highways, these were places tourists and local residents loved to visit.

In 1947, Newton Perry opened an attraction he called Weeki Wachee Springs. Weeki Wachee comes from the Seminole language and means "little spring" or "winding river". A spring is a deep hole or cavern in the ground that constantly fills with pure, clean water. Over one hundred seventeen million gallons of chilly, seventy-two degree water bubbles into the spring every day from underground, filling the spring and flowing out into the river. That's an amazing amount of water each and every day.

Newton's attraction was far from any city, and few cars drove by. He knew he needed more than the spring full of water to make people want to come visit Weeki Wachee. What would people want to see? Mermaids, of course. So he created an enchanted underwater world of mermaids, manatees, turtles and bubbles-lots and lots of bubbles.

He hired pretty, young girls, trained them to swim in costumes, and they performed as mermaids in group ballets with graceful tricks. Girls from all over the world wanted to be one of the famous mermaids. They were able to stay under water for long periods of time by breathing air from special air hoses he made. He also built a seating area for visitors to view the mermaids in their magical world through a special glass wall. Many people came to watch the shows put on by the beautiful mermaids.

In time he added more fun activities. A thrilling flume ride, kiddie pool, kayaking and canoeing, diving and more.

Today, Weeki Wachee Springs is a Florida State Park with fun activities for the whole family, and is open every day of the year.

You can learn more about the park and see photos of the beautiful mermaids at www.weekiwachee.com

Stephen Foster
Father of American Music

Stephen Foster

We all love music. It can excite us and make us want to get up and dance, or it can calm us down and make us feel relaxed to fall asleep. Many songwriters have provided this gift of music for us over the years. But few were able to master the art of bringing melodies and words alive better than the "Father of American Music", Stephen Foster.

Stephen Collins Foster was born in 1826 in Pennsylvania. He was part of a large family, with nine older brothers and sisters. When his father had a hard time making enough money to support everyone, Stephen went to live with other relatives. He missed his family and home, but he was also exposed to different ways of life as a result. These experiences greatly influenced his young life and later his music.

As a young boy he taught himself how to play several different instruments. While living in Pennsylvania with his brother, he wrote his first piece of music, *The Tioga Waltz,* when he was only fourteen-years old. And while living with another brother in Cincinnati, he wrote the song *Oh! Susanna*. Do you know that tune? It was the first piece that he was able to sell to make money.

This was the start of Stephen Foster's long list of songs that people have learned to love over the years like *My Old Kentucky Home, Beautiful Dreamer*, and the favorite, *Jeannie With the Light Brown Hair.* His song *Old Folks At Home* or *Way Down Upon The Suwannee River,* as some call it, became Florida's official state song in 1935. He wrote over two hundred songs during his lifetime.

Today we can enjoy learning more about Stephen Foster by visiting The Stephen Foster Folk Culture Center State Park along the banks of the Suwannee River in White Springs, Florida. The museum honors his accomplishments and features eight dioramas, three-dimensional, animated miniature models enclosed in glass showcases, as well as numerous exhibits about his famous songs.

There is also the two hundred foot tall Stephen Foster Memorial Carillon, a tower containing ninety-seven long, tube shaped bells. Throughout the day the chiming serenades you with favorite Stephen Foster music. What a wonderful way to spend the day. To learn more about Stephen Foster and the park, visit www.floridastateparks.org/stephenfoster

Solomon's Castle

Once upon a time
in a Florida swamp so deep,
stood a bright and shining castle
built by a man quite unique...

Solomon's Castle

Howard Solomon is a unique man, and this is a story about his castle.

Howard was born in 1935 in Rochester, New York. As a youngster he never was fond of school, but discovered that, in addition to his quirky sense of humor, he had very special talents. He grew up to become an internationally known artist and sculptor.

In 1972, after he decided to retire and move to Florida, Howard purchased fifty-five acres of rural property located among orange groves and wilderness approximately one hour northeast of Sarasota near the small town of Ona. It was quiet and woodsy and a perfect retreat to relax, reflect and produce more artwork. Howard decided it was time to create his largest sculpture of all – his family castle.

The 12,000 square foot, three story high medieval style Solomon's Castle took years to build and sits on the banks of Horse Creek, completely surrounded by a moat, a ditch or trench that that is filled with water.

Howard wanted his castle to be special, so he used shiny 22"X34" offset-aluminum printing plates, discarded by a local weekly newspaper, for the outside walls of his castle. Brilliantly gleaming, silver walls. But it didn't stop there. Over eighty beautiful hand-made stained glass windows catch the sun on his castle. And, of course, every window has its own, one of a kind, Howard-style story.

In addition to his family, Howard filled the castle with hundreds of sculptures and works of art. Most show his unique sense of humor and many are created out of junk or trash. Anything you can think of can become a treasure in Howard's talented hands!

Since he had a moat, he decided he might as well have a boat to put in it. Howard spent three years building a sixty-foot replica of a sixteenth century Spanish galleon, complete with murals and stain glass windows. It is now his Boat in the Moat Restaurant.

Would you like to see Solomon's Castle and enjoy a meal "fit for a King" aboard the Boat in the Moat? You can. Howard invites everyone to come tour his fabulous castle. You can find out how by visiting Howard's website at www.solomonscastle.com

The Everglades
Natural Florida

The Everglades

If there's anything in Florida most people have heard about, it's the Everglades. But have you ever stopped to think about just how much you know? Of course, it's located in south Florida, and it's big and wet and has alligators-but that's just the beginning.

Before people started settling in South Florida, the Everglades was a large tropical wilderness covering the entire area from Lake Okeechobee south to the Florida Bay, basically all of the southern tip of the state.

In 1889, a man named George W. Storter, Jr. owned most of the land in an area on the southwest coast of Florida. He is considered the founder of a town simply called Everglade, where he opened a trading post in 1892, and a post office was started in 1895. But it was Barron Collier, a successful Memphis businessman, who is responsible for starting the city we see there today. By 1928, the once sleepy fishing village was bustling with more roads, schools, churches, two hotels, a sawmill, a boat yard, a hospital, a bank, a railroad, and even a jail. Buying up large sections of land, he created Collier County with the town of Everglades (the "s" was added to the name) as County Seat. It wasn't until 1965 that the name was changed to Everglades City.

Everglades City is one of three main entrances into the Everglades National Park, which opened in 1947. It is the third largest National Park in the continental United States covering over 1.5 million acres. It is home to over three-hundred and fifty species or types of birds, including the bald eagle and wood stork; three-hundred species of salt and freshwater fish; fifty types of reptiles including American alligators and crocodiles, and forty different mammals, such as manatees. Approximately one hundred of the existing, endangered Florida Panthers are protected in this unique park.

There is something for everyone to enjoy in the Everglades National Park: camping, hiking, fishing, canoeing and kayaking, biking, bird-watching, boat rides and eco tours in the beautiful, unspoiled wilderness. Are you adventurous? Then an exciting air boat ride is perfect for you. Just hold on!

Would you like to learn more about the everglades and the park? Enjoy the information and photos at www.nps.gov/ever/index.htm

Fascinating Florida Facts

Fasinating Florida Facts

- Ponce de Leon named Florida which means "Feast of Flowers" in Spanish.

- Florida covers 58,560 square miles of area with 4,298 square miles of water.

- Florida is known as "The Sunshine State".

- In 1845, Florida became the 27th state. Tallahassee is Florida's Capitol.

- The first state flag design was adopted in 1899 and its revised design has been in use since 1985.

- Florida has the largest coastline in the continental United States, approximately 1,350 miles.

- There are sixty-seven counties in Florida and the largest city is Jacksonville.

- The largest lake is "Big O" or Lake Okeechobee covering a massive 70 square miles, and is in five counties. It's so big it can be seen from space.

- Stephen Foster wrote the song *The Suwanee River (Old Folks at Home)* in 1851, and it became Florida's state song in 1935.

- The Florida state bird is the Mockingbird, which lives here year round. Did you know they can sing up to 200 songs?

- Flamingos were first documented in Florida in the late 1800's. Although they are not a native Florida bird, they have become a vibrant symbol of the tropical state.

- The state reptile is the Alligator, and the state mammal is the beautiful, yet endangered Florida Panther.

- The State Flower is the orange blossom, and the state drink of course, is orange juice.

- What are your favorite places and things about Florida?

My Color-Full Florida Favorites

(draw your own pictures here)

Made in the USA
Middletown, DE
26 February 2019